The KnitSimple
Book of Knitting Projects for Everyone

The Editors of KnitSimple

The KnitSimple Book of Knitting Projects for Everyone

by the Editors of KnitSimple

Photography by Rose Callahan & Paul Amato

Copyright © 2012 by Mud Puddle, Inc.

Mud Puddle, Inc.
36 W. 25th Street
New York, NY 10010
info@mudpuddleinc.com

ISBN: 978-1-60311-356-4

For KnitSimple:
Copy Editor: Michelle Hainer
Art Director: Matt Shay

Printed in China

Contents

Introduction 4

Glossary 5

Drawstring Hat with Pom Poms 6

Head Scarf 10

Triangular Shawl 13

Jazzy Bands Mittens 16

Wine Bottle Covers 20

Lace Scarf 24

Long Scarf 27

Lace Wristers 30

Cabled Scarf 33

Cabled Wristers 36

Seed Stitch Cardi 40

Beanie & Wristers 44

Braided Cowl 48

Ribbed Cowl 51

Striped Blanket 54

Keyhole Bow Tie 58

Cabled Button Hat 61

INTRODUCTION

There's something seductive about a new knitting project: choosing the perfect pattern, shopping for colorful yarn, casting on the first row of stitches. Perhaps knitting has been passe down to you by a grandmother, aunt, or mother Or, you may be learning to knit for the first time Whatever your skill level, *KnitSimple* will help yo turn a simple skein of yarn into something usef and beautiful.

Our modern world tends to value technology over technique and speed over skill, yet the handcraft of knitting thrives. Many find pleasur in the tactile work of slipping soft yarn back and forth across needles. Knitting becomes an act of meditation or relaxation, a way to relieve stress. Though the craft originated in ancient Egypt, th popularity of knitting soars today.

Within these pages you'll find 17 needlecraft projects to satisfy a myriad of creative yearning from wine bottle covers to warm winter wraps. *KnitSimple* offers beginner, easy, and intermedi patterns that will inspire you for months on end

Whether knitting for yourself, family member or friends, *KnitSimple* contains all the instructio you need for beautiful hand knit garments, accessories, and gifts.

For new knitters, reading patterns may seem like studying a foreign language. But once you become familiar with the standard abbreviations often used, you'll be able to decipher patterns in no time! Here are some common symbols and abbreviations you will come across. If a pattern requires a particular skill, the author will usually include this in a glossary within the pattern.

Glossary

( ) – Work instructions in between parentheses in the place directed.

[ ] – Work instructions in between brackets as many times as directed.

* – Repeat instructions following the asterisk as directed.

beg – Beginning

bet – Between

BO – Bind off

CC – Contrasting color

ch – Chain, using a crochet hook

cn – Cable needle

CO – Cast on

dpns or dp – Double-pointed needles

foll – Follows

inc 1 – Increase one stitch

k – Knit

kfb – A method used to increase a stitch. Knit one stitch in the front and then in the back before slipping to the right needle. This is also known as a bar increase.

k2tog – Knit two stitches together

LC – Left cross, as to knit a cable

p – Purl

pm – Place marker

psso – Pass slipped stitch over. Slip a stitch, knit a stitch, pass the slipped stitch over. Also called SKP.

p2tog – Purl two stitches together

pu – Pick up stitches

M1 – Make one. This means to increase a stitch. If the method isn't specified you can do this however you like, usually by picking up a loop between two stitches and knitting into the back of it or knitting into the front and back of a stitch that is on your needle (kfb).

MC – Main color

RC – Right cross, as to knit a cable

rem – Remaining

rep – Repeat

rib – Vertical columns of knit and purl stitches as in k2, p2 ribbing.

rnd (s) – Round. When knitting in the round using a circular needle (as for hats) a row is called a round.

RS – Right side of work, as in the side that will face outward on the finished garment.

sc – Single crochet

sk – Skip

sl – Slip a stitch

slip knot – An adjustable loop, usually used to begin casting on.

SKP – Slip, knit, pass. Slip a stitch, knit a stitch, pass the slipped stitch over.

sk2p – Slip 1, k2tog, pass slipped stitch over

SSK – Slip, slip, knit. Slip one stitch, slip one stitch, then knit the slipped stitches together.

Sts – Stitches

St st – Stockinette stitch

tbl – Through back loop

yo – Yarnover. Wrap the yarn around the right needle, then knit the next stitch.

WS – Wrong side of work, as in the side that won't show on the finished garment.

Drawstring Hat with Pom Pom

Design by Tanis Gray

Whether you're wrapping yarn around your fingers or using a store-bought form, it's easy to plump up a perky pompom.

MATERIALS

- Approximately 150 yds of a worsted weight yarn
- One pair size 6 (4mm) knitting needles OR SIZE TO OBTAIN GAUGE
- Size G/6 (4mm) crochet hook

Used in Photo: Alpine 10 Ply by Naturally NZ/Fiber Trends, 7oz/200g skeins, each approximately 364yd/333m (pure New Zealand wool). 1 skein each in #2003 cranberry (MC) and #2008 turquoise (CC)

Note: Sized for small, medium, large. Shown in size small.

Knit Wits

To keep your finished projects looking new, add one or two drops of glycerin into the wash water to smooth the yarn and keep your garment from pilling or bunching.

TEMPLATE

Template 2"/5cm

MEASUREMENTS

- Circumference 18 (20, 22)"/45.5 (51, 56)cm

GAUGE

- 22 sts and 36 rows to 4"/10cm over k2, p2 rib using size 6 (4mm) needles (slightly stretched).
- TAKE TIME TO CHECK YOUR GAUGE.

PROJECT: HAT

- With MC, cast on 100 (112, 120) stitches. Work even in k2, p2 rib until piece measures 9 (9½, 10"/23 (24, 25.5)cm from beg. Bind off loosely in rib.

FINISHING

- Sew back seam.

BOTTOM EDGING

- With RS of bottom edge facing and crochet hook, join CC with a sl st in back seam.
- Rnd 1 (RS) Ch 1, making sure that work lies flat, sc evenly around entire edge, join rnd with a sl st in first sc. Fasten off.

TOP EDGING

- With RS of top edge facing and crochet hook, join CC with a sl st in back seam.
- Cont to work as for bottom edging.

DRAWSTRING

- Cut six 34"/86.5cm long strands of CC. Gather strands tog, ends even.
- Make an overhand knot 5"/12.5cm from one end. Divide strands into three 2-strand groups. Braid for 24"/61cm from base of knot.
- Make an overhand knot at base of braid. Thread one end of braid into yarn needle. Beg and ending at center front, use yarn needle to weave braid under and over every knit rib of rib pat.

POM POMS (MAKE 2)

- Using CC, make two 2"/5cm diameter pom poms. Sew pom poms to ends of braid.

Head Scarf

• •

Design by Linda Cyr

Experiment with different decreases as you make progress on a simple head covering perfect for a breezy day.

MATERIALS

- Approximately 200 yds of ribbon yarn
- One size 7 (4.5mm) circular needle, 29"/74cm long O SIZE TO OBTAIN GAUGE
- 1 set of size 7 double-pointed needles

Used in Photo: Sonata by The Great Adirondack Yarn Co. 3oz/85g skeins, each approximately 200yd/183m (nylon). 1 skein in irish cream

MEASUREMENTS

- Approximately 18"/45.5cm wide x 13"/33cm at longes point (without ties)

GAUGE

- 20 sts and 28 rows to 4"/10cm over St st using size 7 (4.5mm) needles.
- TAKE TIME TO CHECK YOUR GAUGE.

Note: A circular needle is used to accommodate the large number of sts. Work back and forth in rows.

PROJECT: HEAD SCARF

- Cast on 91 sts.
- Row 1 (RS) ssk, k to last 2 sts, k2tog. Row 2 Purl.
- Rep rows 1 and 2 until 3 sts rem, ending with a WS row.
- Next row sl 1, k2tog, psso. Bind off.
- TIES (make 2) With dpn, cast on 4 sts. Work I-cord as foll: *Next row (RS) k4. Slide sts back to beg of needle so that next row is a RS row; rep from *until tie measures 10"/25.5cm long. Bind off.

FINISHING

- Sew ends of ties to long edge of scarf, letting edge roll around ties.

TAKE
TIME
TO CHECK
YOUR
GAUGE

Triangular Shawl

Design by Linda Cyr

Begin this shawl with one stitch, then increase stitches on either side to create a triangle as wide as desired. Shown on page 15.

MATERIALS

- Approximately 628 yds of a bulky weight yarn
- One size 10 (6mm) circular needle 29"/ 74cm long OR SIZE TO OBTAIN GAUGE

Used in Photo: Giotto by Colinette, 3½oz/100g skeins, each approximately 153yd/ 144m (cotton/rayon/nylon). 4 skeins in #137 banwy

MEASUREMENTS

- Approximately 62"/157.5cm wide x 40"/101.5cm at longest point

GAUGE

- 13 sts and 20 rows to 4"/10cm over St st using size 10 (6mm) needle.
- TAKE TIME TO CHECK YOUR GAUGE.

Note: A circular needle is used to accommodate the large number of sts. Work back and forth in rows.

PROJECT: SHAWL

- Cast on 3 stitches
- Row 1 (RS) K1, yo, k2
- Row 2 Purl.
- Row 3 K1, yo, k to within 1 stitch of last stitch, yo, k1.
- Rep rows 2 and 3 until there are 201 sts. Piece measures approx 62"/157.5cm wide and 40"/101.5cm (measured at center)
- Loosely bind off all stitches.

Jazzy Band Mittens

Design by Charlotte Perry

Try variations to this basic mitten pattern—solid color cuffs and thumbs, wide stripes, a self-striping yarn—the sky is the limit!

MATERIALS

- Approximately 624 yards of a worsted weight yarn
- One set of size 6 (4mm) double-pointed needles OR SIZE TO OBTAIN GAUGE
- Safety pin or small stitch holder

Used in Photo: TLC Essentials by Coats & Clark, 6oz/170g skeins, each approximately 312yd/285m (acrylic). 1 skein each in #2254 persimmon (A) and #2220 butter (B)

Basic two-striped mitten sized for children, women, men. Shown in women's size.

FINISHED MEASUREMENTS

- Length from wrist to fingertips 7 (10, 11)"/18 (25.5, 28)cm
- Wrist circumference 5¼ (6½, 7½)"/13.5 (16.5, 19)cm

GAUGE

- 20 sts and 28 rows to 4"/10cm over St st using size 6 (4mm) needles.
- TAKE TIME TO CHECK YOUR GAUGE.

PROJECT: MITTENS

Basic mitten sized for children, women, men.

FINISHED MEASUREMENTS

- Length from wrist to fingertips 7 (10, 11)"/18 (25.5, 28)cm
- Wrist circumference 5¼ (6½, 7½)"/13.5 (16.5, 19)cm

GAUGE

- 20 sts and 28 rows to 4"/10cm over St st using size 6 (4mm) needles.
- TAKE TIME TO CHECK YOUR GAUGE.

LEFT MITTEN

- Cast on 8 (10, 12) sts on first dpn, 8 (10, 12) sts on 2nd dpn, 8 (10, 12) sts on 3rd dpn and 8 (10, 12) sts on 4th dpn—32 (40, 48) sts.
- Pm to mark beg of rnd and join. Work in k1, p1 rib for 2 (3, 3)"/5 (7.5, 7.5)cm.
- Change to St st and work even for 3 rows.

BASE OF THUMB SHAPING

- Rnd 1 K12 (16, 20), M1, k2, M1, k rem sts to end—34 (42, 50) sts. Rnds 2 and 3 Knit.

- Rnd 4 K12 (16, 20), M1, k4, M1, k rem sts to end—36 (44, 52) sts.
- Rnds 5 and 6 Knit.
- Rnd 7 K12 (16, 20), M1, k6, M1, k rem sts to end—38 (46, 54) sts.
- Rnds 8 and 9 Knit.
- Rnd 10 K12 (16, 20), M1, k8, M1, k rem sts to end—40 (48, 56) sts.
- Rnds 11 and 12 Knit.
- Rnd 13 K12 (16, 20), M1, k10, M1, k rem sts to end—42 (50, 58) sts.

FOR WOMEN'S AND MEN'S SIZES ONLY

- Rnds 14 and 15 Knit.
- Rnd 16 K (16, 20), M1, k12, M1, k rem sts to end—(52, 60) sts.
- Rnd 17 Knit.

FOR MEN'S SIZE ONLY

- Rnds 18 and 19 Knit.
- Rnd 20 K20, M1, k14, M1, k rem sts to end—62 sts.
- Rnd 21 Knit.

FOR ALL SIZES

- Next rnd K12 (16, 20), place next 12 (14, 16) sts on a holder (either a contrast color strand of yarn or a small stitch holder) for thumb, cast on 2 sts, k to end of rnd—32 (40, 48) sts.
- Cont in St st on 32 (40, 48) sts for hand of mitten until piece is 5½ (8½, 9½)"/ 14 (21.5, 24)cm, or until hand is long enough to cover index fingernail.

MITTEN TOP SHAPING

- Rnd 1 K1, SKP, k10 (14, 18), k2tog, k2, SKP, k10 (14, 18), k2tog, k1—28 (36, 44) sts.
- Rnd 2 K1, SKP, k8 (12, 16), k2tog, k2, SKP, k8 (12, 16) sts, k2tog, k1—24 (32, 40) sts.
- Rnd 3 K1, SKP, k6 (10, 14), k2tog, k2, SKP, k6 (10, 14), k2tog, k1—20 (28, 36) sts.
- Rnd 4 K1, SKP, k4 (8, 12), k2tog, k2, SKP, k4 (8, 12), k2tog, k1—16 (24, 32) sts.
- Rnd 5 K1, SKP, k2 (6, 10), k2tog, k2, SKP, k2 (6, 10), k2tog, k1—12 (20, 28) sts.

FOR WOMEN'S AND MEN'S SIZES ONLY

- Rnd 6 K1, SKP, k(4, 8), k2tog, k2, SKP, k(4, 8), k2tog, k1—(16, 24) sts.
- Rnd 7 K1, SKP, k(2, 6), k2tog, k2, SKP, k(2, 6), k2tog, k1—(12, 20) sts.
- For men's size only:
  - Rnd 8 K1, SKP, k4, k2tog, k2, SKP, k4, k2tog, k1—16 sts.
  - Rnd 9 K1, SKP, k2, k2tog, k2, SKP, k2, k2tog, k1—12 sts.

FOR ALL SIZES

- Last rnd K1, SKP, k2tog, k2, SKP, k2tog, k1—8 sts.
- Cut yarn, draw yarn end through rem 8 sts and bind off.

THUMB

- Pick up 5 (6, 7) sts from 12 (14, 16) sts on holder with first dpn, 5 (6, 7) sts with 2nd dpn and 2 sts with 3rd dpn; pick up and knit 2 sts from hand of mitten—14 (16, 18) sts.
- Work even in St st until thumb measures 1¼ (2, 2¼)"/3.5 (5, 6)cm, or long enough to cover half of thumbnail.
- Next row [K2tog, k1] 4 (5, 6) times, k2 (1, 0)—10 (11, 12) sts.
- Next row [K2 tog] 5 (5, 6) times, k0 (1, 0)— 5 (6, 6) sts.
- Next row [K2 tog] 2 (3, 3) times, k1 (0, 0)—3 sts.
- Cut yarn, draw yarn end through rem 3 sts and bind off.

RIGHT MITTEN

- Work as for left mitten except position base of thumb as follows:
- Rnd 1 K18 (22, 26), M1, k2, M1, k rem sts to end—34 (42, 50) sts. Shape remainder of thumb base and mitten as for left mitten.

PROJECT-5

Easy

Wine Bottle Covers

• •

Design by Faith Hale

Two different bottle cozies keep your liquid refreshments well insulated.

MATERIALS

- Approximately 300 yds of a DK weight yarn
- One set of size 7 double-pointed needles OR SIZE TO OBTAIN GAUGE
- 2 size 7 (4.5mm) double-pointed needles (for I-cord)

Used in Photo: Silk Blend by Manos del Uruguay/Fairmount Fibers, Ltd, 1¾oz/50g skeins, each approximately 150yd/135m (wool/silk). 1 skein each in #3043 juniper (blue A) and #3068 citric (green B)

SIZE

- Fits average wine bottle.

MEASUREMENTS

BOTTLE COVER A

- Circumference (unstretched) Approximately 7"/18cm
- Length 12"/30.5cm

BOTTLE COVER B

- Circumference Approximately 9½"/24cm
- Length 7½"/19cm

GAUGE

- 20 sts and 32 rows over k3, p2 rib (unstretched) using size 7 (4.5mm) needles.
- 20 sts and 30 rows over garter st using size 7 (4.5mm) needles.
- TAKE TIME TO CHECK YOUR GAUGE.

K3, P2 RIB

- (over a multiple of 5 sts, plus 2)
- Row 1 *K3, p2; rep from * , end k2.
- Row 2 P2, *k2, p3; rep from * to end.
- Rep rows 1 and 2 for k3, p2 rib.

NOTES:
1) Bottle cover A (blue) is worked from the top down.
2) Bottle cover B (green) is worked from side to side.

PROJECT: BOTTLE COVER A

- With A and straight needles, cast on 57 sts. Work in k3, p2 rib until piece measures 12"/30.5cm from beg.
- Bind off tightly, as foll: K1, k2tog, *pass first st over 2nd, k2 tog; rep from * to end.

I-CORD TIE

- With 2 dpns and B, cast on 4 sts. *Knit one row. Without turning work, slide the sts back to beg of the row. Pull yarn tightly from the end of the row. Rep from * until cord is 16"/40.5cm long.

FINISHING

- Sew side seam, forming tube. Tack I-cord in place 2"/5cm from cast-on edge.

PROJECT: BOTTLE COVER B

BODY

- With B and straight needles, cast on 37 sts. Work in garter st (k every row) for 5 rows.
- Next (eyelet) row k2, k2tog, yo, k to end. Cont in garter st, rep eyelet row every 6th row until piece measures 11"/28cm from beg. Bind off.

BASE PIECE

- With B and straight needles, cast on 4 sts.
- Next (inc) row K1, inc 1 st in next st, k to last 2 sts, inc 1 st in next st, k 1—6 sts.
- Work In garter st rep inc row every row 4 times more—14 sts.
- K 6 rows.
- Rep inc row—16 sts. K 4 rows.
- Next (dec) row K1, k2tog, k to last 3 sts, k2tog, k1—14 sts. K 6 rows.
- Rep dec row every row 5 times—4 sts. Bind off.

FINISHING

- Fold body piece in half, sew cast-on end to bound-off end. Sew base piece to lower end.

TWISTED CORD

- Cut strand of B approximately 45"/114cm long. Fold in half and twist until it begins to twist back on itself. Knot each end and thread through eyelets.

Lace Scarf

• •

Design by Lois Young

MATERIALS

- Approximately 600 yds of a DK weight yarn
- One pair size 7 (4.5mm) needles OR SIZE TO OBTAIN GAUGE
- Stitch marker

Used in Photo: Serena by Manos del Uruguay/Fairmount Fibers, Inc, 1¾oz/50g skeins, each approximately 170yd/155m (alpaca/cotton). 4 skeins in #2457 tide (blue)

MEASUREMENTS

- 15 x 67"/38 x 70cm (without fringe)

GAUGE

- 18 sts and 26 rows to 4"/10cm over lace pat using size 7 (4.5mm) needles after blocking.
- TAKE TIME TO CHECK YOUR GAUGE.

NOTE: Slip the first stitch of each row with yarn in front, then bring yarn to back between first and 2nd sts and knit.

LACE PATTERN (MULTIPLE OF 4 STS)

- Row 1 sl 1, k3, *k2, yo, k2tog; rep from *to last 4 sts, end k3, k1 tbl.
- Rep row 1 for lace pat.

PROJECT: SCARF

- Cast on 76 sts loosely.
- Row 1 (WS) Sl 1 st, k to last st, k1 tbl.
- Rows 2-7 Rep row 1.

Note: Mark next row for RS.

- Work in lace pat until piece measures 66¼"/168cm from beg.
- Next 7 rows Work rows 1-7 same as beg of scarf.
- Bind off loosely.

FINISHING

- Block scarf.

FRINGE

- Cut 20½"/52cm lengths of yarn.
- Thread 4 strands through yarn needle; insert needle into edge stitch and pull yarn halfway through.
- Remove needle, line up ends of strands, then tie fringe into single knot close to edge of wrap.
- Tie one 4-strand fringe at each corner, and at each end of solid columns of sts. Tie 2 more knots in fringe at 2"/5cm apart.
- Trim ends of fringe to measure 2"/5cm below final knot.

Easy

Long Scarf

Design by Rosemary Drysdale

hown on page 29

MATERIALS

- Approximately 400 yds of a worsted weight yarn
- One pair size 7 (4.5mm) needles OR SIZE TO OBTAIN GAUGE
- Safety pin

Used in Photo: Eco Cotton by Debbie Bliss/KFI, 1¾oz/50g skeins, each approximately 99yd/75m (organic cotton). 4 skeins in #614 denim blue

MEASUREMENTS

- Approximately 7 x 56"/17.5 x 142cm

GAUGE

- 18 sts and 24 rows to 4"/10cm over St st using size 7 (4.5 mm) needles.
- TAKE TIME TO CHECK YOUR GAUGE.

STRIPE PATTERN

- *10 rows St st, 10 rows rev St st; rep from * (20 rows) for stripe pat.

PROJECT: SCARF

- Cast on 3 sts and work in stripe pat as foll:
    - Row 1 (RS) Kfb, k to last st, kfb.
    - Row 2 Purl.
    - Rows 3-10 Rep rows 1 and 2 four times—13 sts.
    - Row 11 (K1, p1) in first st, p to last st, (p1, k1 tbl) in last st.
    - Row 12 Knit.
    - Rows 13-20 Rep rows 11 and 12 four times—23 sts.

Note: Place safety pin on RS of work. Keep a careful count of the rows to determine when to change from St st to rev St st in the stripe pat.

- Rows 21-40 Rep rows 1-20 once—43 sts.
- Piece measures approximately 7"/17.5cm wide (measured along side edge). Cont to work even in stripe pat as foll: Next row (RS) Inc in first st, work to last 2 sts, k2tog.
- Work 1 row even.
- Rep last 2 rows until the long side measures approximately 56"/142cm, end with a WS row.
- Dec row (RS) Bind off 2 sts, work to last 2 sts, k2tog.
- Work 1 row even.
- Rep last 2 rows until all sts have been decreased.
- Fasten off.

PROJECT-8

Median

Lace Wristers

Design by Kirsten Kapur

Sized for Women's.

MATERIALS

- Approximately 150 yds of a worsted weight yarn
- One set (5) size 5 (3.75mm) double-pointed needles OR SIZE TO OBTAIN GAUGE

Used in Photo: Eden Silk by Universal Yarn, 1oz/50g skeins, each approximately 153yd/140m (wool/silk). 1 skein in #12 sea

MEASUREMENTS

- Circumference Approximately 6"/15cm, (will stretch to fit up to 9"/23cm)
- Length 6"/15cm

GAUGE

- 26 sts and 34 rows to 4"/10cm over lace chart using size 5 (3.75mm) needles.
- TAKE TIME TO CHECK YOUR GAUGE.

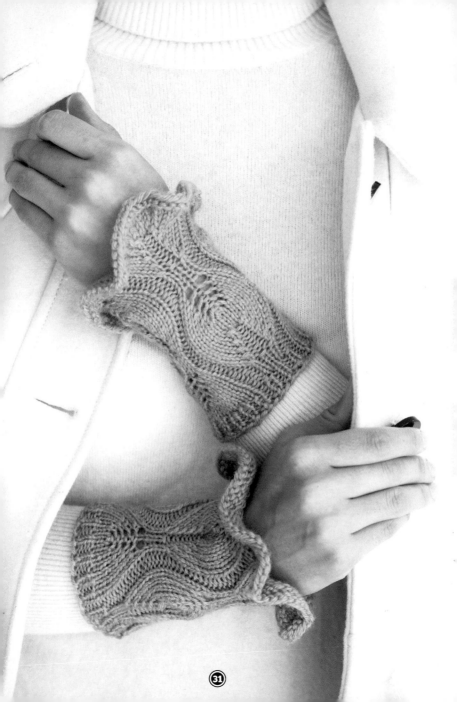

PROJECT: WRISTERS

RUFFLE

- With dpns, cast on 80 sts.
- Divide sts evenly over 4 dpns (20 sts on each dpn). Place marker (pm) and join, being careful not to twi‹ sts. P1 rnd, k4 rnds.
- Next rnd *K2tog; rep from *around—40 sts.

BEG CHART

- Rnd 1 Work 20-st rep chart 2 times around. When 2‹ rnds of chart pat are complete, work rnds 1-14 once more.
- Work in k1, p1 rib for 4 rnds.
- Bind off loosely.

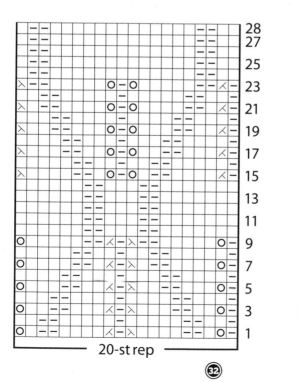

STITCH KEY

- ☐ k on RS
- ⊟ p on RS
- ⊙ yo
- ⊠ k2tog
- ⊠ ssk

20-st rep

Cabled Scarf

Design by Coralie Meslin

hown on page 35

MATERIALS

- Approximately 410 yds of a bulky weight yarn
- One pair size 10½ (6.5mm) needles OR SIZE TO OBTAIN GAUGE.
- Cable needle (cn)

Used in Photo: Big Baby by Alpaca With A Twist
3½oz/100g skeins, each approximately 82yd/75m
(baby alpaca). 5 skeins in ##3003 carnival red

MEASUREMENTS

- Approximately 7½ x 60"/19 x 152.5cm

GAUGE

- 20 sts and 16 rows to 4"/10cm over k2, p2 rib (unstretched) using size 10½ (6.5mm) needles.
- TAKE TIME TO CHECK YOUR GAUGE.

STITCH GLOSSARY

- 16-st RC Slip 8 sts to cn and hold to back, [k2, p2] twice, work sts from cn as foll: [k2, p2] twice.
- 16-st LC Slip 8 sts to cn and hold to front, [k2, p2] twice, work sts from cn as follows: [k2, p2] twice.

PROJECT: SCARF

- Cast on 40 sts.
- Work k2, p2 rib for 12 rows.
- Rep row 2 for k2, p2 rib for 10 rows more.

BEG CABLE PATTERN

- Row 1 (RS) *K2, p2; rep from * to end.
- Row 2 and all WS rows K the knit sts and p the purl sts.
- Row 3 K2, p2, work 16-st LC, *k2, p2 rep from * to end.
- Rows 5-12 K the knit sts and p the purl sts.
- Row 13 [K2, p2] 5 times, work 16-st RC, k2, p2.
- Rows 14-20 K the knit sts and p the purl sts.
- Rep rows 1-2 for a total of 11 times.
- Work 7 rows more in k2, p2 rib.
- Bind off in rib.

Cabled Wristers

Design by Kirsten Kapur

Sized for Women's.

MATERIALS

- Approximately 104 yds of a worsted weight yarn
- One pair size 7 (4.5mm) needles OR SIZE TO OBTAIN GAUGE
- Cable needle (cn)
- 10½"/12mm buttons

Used in Photo: Supermerino by Artyarns, 1¾oz/50gr skeins each approximately 104yd/95m. 1 skein in #260 ochre.

MEASUREMENTS

- Circumference (buttoned) 7½"/19cm
- Length (wrist to fingers) 7"/18cm

GAUGE

- 20 sts and 35 rows to 4"/10cm over St st using size 1 (6mm) needles.
- TAKE TIME TO CHECK YOUR GAUGE.

Knit Wits

When learning to knit, choose inexpensive acrylic yarns. You'll make mistakes, so it's best not to buy costly yarns on your first knitting projects.

STITCH GLOSSARY

- 4-st RC: Sl 2 sts to cn and hold to back, k2, k2 from cn.
- 4-st LC: sl 2 sts to cn and hold to front, k2, k2 from cn.

PROJECT: LEFT WRISTER

- With size 7 (4.5mm) needles, cast on 35 sts. Knit rows. Next (buttonhole) row (WS) K3, [yo, k2tog, k5] 4 times, yo, k2tog, k2.
- Knit 2 rows.

BEG BACK OF HAND

- Row 1 (RS) k10 for wristband, p2, [k4, p2] 3 times, k5.
- Rows 2 and 4 k7, [p4, k2] 3 times, k10.
- Row 3 k10, p2 [4-st RC, p2] 3 times, k5.
- Rows 5 and 6 Rep rows 1 and 2.
- Rep rows 1-6 4 times more, then rep rows 1-5 once more.
- Knit 1 row.

THUMB OPENING

- Next row (RS) k12, bind off 10 sts, k to end.
- Next row k13, cast on 10 sts over bound-off sts, k to end.

PALM

- Work in garter st (k every row) until piece measures 3½"/9cm from thumb opening.
- Bind off.

PROJECT: RIGHT WRISTER

- Cast on and work as for Left Wrister, end with buttonhole row.

BEG BACK OF HAND

- Row 1 (RS) K5, p2, [k4, p2] 3 times, k10 for wristband.
- Rows 2 and 4 k12, [p4, k2] 3 times, k5.
- Row 3 k5, p2 [4-st LC, p2] 3 times, k10.
- Rows 5 and 6 Rep rows 1 and 2.
- Rep rows 1-6 4 times more, then rep rows 1-5 once more.
- Knit 1 row.

THUMB OPENING

- Next row (RS) k13, bind off 10 sts, k to end of row.
- Next row k12, cast on 10 sts over bound-off sts, k to end.

PALM

- Work as for Left Wrister.

FINISHING

- Sew on buttons opposite buttonholes.

Knit Wits

In order to keep light colored knitting projects clean and from touching the floor while you're working, place the garment in a pillowcase in your lap as you knit.

Seed Stitch Cardi

Design by Helene Rush

Sized for X-small, small, medium, large, 1X, 2X. Shown in size X-small.

MATERIALS

- Approximately 1417 yds of a worsted weight yarn
- Size 8 (5mm) circular needle, 32"/81cm long OR SIZE TO OBTAIN GAUGE
- Stitch markers

Used in Photo: Brae Tweed by Knit One, Crochet Too, Inc., 1¾oz/50g skeins, each approximately 100yd/99m (wool/ llama/bamboo/donegal). 6 (7, 8, 9, 10, 10) skeins in #10 lichen

MEASUREMENTS

- Bust (closed) 36 (39, 42, 45, 48, 51)"/91.5 (99, 106.5, 114.5, 122, 129.5)cm
- Length 21 (21½, 21¾, 22½, 23½, 24¼)"/53.5 (54.5, 55, 57, 59.5, 61.5)cm
- Upper arm 13 (14½, 16, 17½, 19, 20½)"/33 (37, 40.5, 44.5, 48, 52)cm

GAUGE

- 18 sts and 26 rows to 4"/10cm over St st using size 8 (5mm) circular needle.
- TAKE TIME TO CHECK YOUR GAUGE.

Introduci

alph Lau

Watchm

Note: Yoke and body are worked back and forth in one piece from the neck down.

STITCH GLOSSARY

- Kfb: inc 1 by knitting into the front and back of the next st.

SEED STITCH

- Row 1 (RS) K1, *p1, k1; rep from * to end.
- Row 2 K the purl sts and p the knit sts.
- Rep row 2 for seed st.

YOKE

- Beg at neck edge, cast on 111 (119, 127, 135, 143, 151) sts.
- Work in seed st for 2 rows.
- Next (set-up and buttonhole) row (RS) Work in seed st over first 21 (22, 23, 24, 25, 26) sts (left front), pm, k2, pm, work in seed st over next 13 (15, 17, 19, 21, 23) sts (left cap sleeve), pm, k2, pm, work in seed st over next 35 (37, 39, 41, 43, 45) sts (back), pm, k2, pm, work in seed st over next 13 (15, 17, 19, 21, 23) sts (right cap sleeve), pm, k2, pm, work to end of row in seed st (right front)—111 (119, 127, 135, 143, 151) sts.
- Next row *Work in seed st to next marker, sl marker, p2, sl marker; rep from * 3 times more, work in seed st to end.
- Next (inc) row (RS) *Work in seed st to next marker, yo, sl marker, k sl marker, yo; rep from * 3 times more, work in seed st to end.
- Next row *Work in seed st to next marker, sl marker, p2, sl marker; rep from * 3 times more, work in seed st to end. Rep last 2 rows 17
- (19, 21, 23, 25, 27) times more—2 (279, 303, 327, 351, 375) sts. AT THE SAME TIME, work 5 more buttonholes, spacing them every ½ (2½, 2½, 2¾, 2¾, 2¾)"/6.5 (6.5, 6.5, 7, 7, 7)cm.

DIVIDE FOR BODY AND CAP SLEEVES

- Next row (RS) Working in and binding off in seed st, and dropping old markers, work as follows: work 5 sts (front band), pm, work next 36 (39, 42, 45, 48, 51) sts (left front), bind off next 50 (56, 62, 68, 74, 80) sts (left cap sleeve), cast on 8 (8, 10, 10, 12, 12) sts (left underarm), work next 73 (79, 85, 91, 97, 103) sts (back), bind off next 51 (57, 63, 69, 75, 81) sts (right cap sleeve), cast on 8 (8, 10, 10, 12, 12) sts (right underarm), work next 35 (38, 41, 44, 47, 50) sts (right front), pm work last 5 sts (front band)—171 (183, 199, 211, 227, 239) sts.

BODY

- Next row (WS) Working in seed st, work first 44 (47, 51, 54, 58, 61) sts, pm, work next 81 (87, 95, 101,

109, 115) sts, pm, work last 44 (47, 51, 54, 58, 61) sts. Cont in seed st on all sts for 1"/2.5cm, end with a WS row.

- Next row (RS) Work in seed st over first 5 sts, sl marker, k to next marker, sl marker, work in seed st over last 5 sts.
- Next row Work in seed st over first 5 sts, sl marker, p to next marker, sl marker, work in seed st over last 5 sts.
- Cont to work in this way, keeping 5 sts each front edge in seed st and rem sts in St st, until piece measures 2"/5cm from underarm cast-on, end with a WS row.

SHAPE SIDES

- Next (inc) row (RS) *Work to 1 st before next marker, kfb, sl marker, kfb; rep from * once more.

- Rep last row every 2"/5cm 5 times more—193 (205, 221, 233, 249, 261) sts.
- Work even over these sts in seed st and St st as established, until piece measures 13 (13, 12½, 12½, 12½, 12½)"/33 (33, 31.5, 31.5, 31.5, 31.5) cm from underarm cast-on, end with a WS row.

LOWER EDGE BAND

- Cont in seed st on all sts for 1"/2.5cm.
- Bind off all sts loosely in seed st.

FINISHING

- Block piece to measurements.
- Sew on buttons.

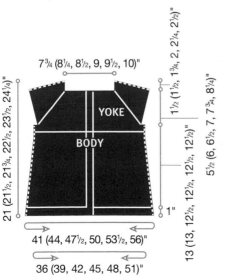

7¾ (8¼, 8½, 9, 9½, 10)"

YOKE

BODY

21 (21½, 21¾, 22½, 23½, 24¼)"

1½ (1½, 1¾, 2, 2¼, 2½)"

5½ (6, 6½, 7, 7, 7¾, 8¼)"

13 (13, 12½, 12½, 12½, 12½)"

1"

41 (44, 47½, 50, 53½, 56)"

36 (39, 42, 45, 48, 51)"

Beanie & Wristers

Design by Renee Lorion

PROJECT: BEANIE

MATERIALS

- Approximately 232 yds of a bulky weight yarn
- Size 10 (6mm) circular needle, 16"/40cm long OR SIZE TO OBTAIN GAUGE
- Six stitch markers, yarn needle

Used in Photo: Chunky by Claudia Hand Painted Yarns, 3 ½oz/100g skeins, each approximately 116yd/106m (wool). 1 skein in #8080 limeade

MEASUREMENTS

- Circumference approximately 15"/38cm
- Length approximately 8½"/21.5cm

GAUGE

- 16 sts and 20 rows to 4"/10cm over St st using size 10 (6mm) needle.
- TAKE TIME TO CHECK YOUR GAUGE.

HAT

- Cast on 60 sts. Join, being careful not to twist sts, and place marker (pm) for beg of rnd.
- Purl 8 rnds.
- Change to St st (k every rnd) and work until piece measures 6½"/16.5cm from beg.
- Next rnd [K10, pm] 5 times, k10.

SHAPE CROWN

- Rnd 1 *k to 2 sts before marker, k2tog, sl marker; rep from * around—54 sts.
- Rnd 2 Knit.
- Rep [rnds 1 and 2] 7 times more—12 sts.
- Next rnd *k2tog; rep from * around, removing markers—6 sts. Cut yarn leaving long tail.
- Thread tail through yarn needle and draw through open sts.

PROJECT: WRISTERS

MATERIALS

- One set (4) size 10 (6mm) double-pointed needles OR SIZE TO OBTAIN GAUGE
- Stitch markers, stitch holder or scrap yarn

Used in Photo: Chunky by Claudia Hand Painted Yarns, 3 ½oz/100g skeins, each approximately 116yd/106m (wool). 1 skein in #8080 limeade

MEASUREMENTS

- Circumference (above thumb) 5¾"/14.5cm
- Length approximately 9½"/24cm

GAUGE

- 16 sts and 20 rows to 4"/10cm over St st using size 10 (6mm) needles.
- TAKE TIME TO CHECK YOUR GAUGE.

WRISTERS

- With dpns, cast on 24 sts. Join, being careful not to twist sts, and pm for beg of rnd. Purl 6 rnds.
- Change to St st (k every rnd) and work until piece measures 4"/10cm from beg.
- Next rnd K1, pm, k1, pm, k to end of rnd.

BEG THUMB GUSSET

- Next (inc) rnd K to next marker, sl marker, M1, k to next marker, M1, sl marker, k to end of rnd—26 sts.
- K 1 rnd.
- Cont in St st, rep inc rnd 4 times more—34 sts (11 sts between markers). Work even until piece measures 7"/18cm from beg.
- Next rnd K1, place next 11 sts on holder or scrap yarn for thumb, k to end of rnd—23 sts.
- Work 6 rnds even.
- Purl 4 rnds.
- Bind off.

THUMB

- Arrange 11 thumb sts on 3 dpn. Rejoin yarn at thumb opening, k11, pick up and k 2 sts— 13 sts.
- Next rnd K11, k2tog—12 sts.
- purl one rnd.
- Next rnd P10, p2tog.
- purl one rnd.
- Bind off knitwise.

Knit Wits

Consider casting on with a needle one size larger than you plan to knit with. This is especially helpful if you tend to cast on too tightly, as it makes it easier to begin a new project.

Easy

Braided Crowl

Design by Faith Hale

MATERIALS

- Approximately 261 yds of a bulky weight yarn
- One pair size 10½ (6.5mm) needles OR SIZE TO OBTAIN GAUGE

Used in Photo: Ariosa by Classic Elite Yarns, 1¾oz/50g ball, each approximately 87yd/80m (wool/cashmere). 3 balls in #4820 milkweed

MEASUREMENTS

- Circumference 27"/68.5cm
- Length 6"/15cm

GAUGE

- 12 sts and 16 rows to 4"/10cm over St st using size 10 ½ (6.5mm) needles.
- TAKE TIME TO CHECK YOUR GAUGE.

PROJECT: COWL

- Strip (make 3)
- Cast on 11 sts.
- Row 1 *kfb; rep from * to end—22 sts.
- Work in St st (k on RS, p on WS) until piece measures 33"/83.5cm from beg.
- Next row *K2tog; rep from * to end—11 sts.
- Bind off. Sew long edges of strip tog, forming tube.

FINISHING

- Braid 3 strips tog loosely. Sew cast-on and bound-off edges tog.

TAKE
TIME
TO CHECK
YOUR
GAUGE

Ribbed Cowl

Design by Renee Lorion

MATERIALS

- Approximately 590 yds of a DK weight yarn
- One pair size 6 (4mm) needles OR SIZE TO OBTAIN GAUGE

Used in Photo: Symphony by Prism, 2oz/57g skeins, each approximately 118yd/108m (wool/cashmere/nylon). 5 skeins in denali

MEASUREMENTS

- Circumference 34"/86.5cm
- Length 20"/51cm

GAUGE

- 20 sts and 26 rows to 4"/10cm over St st using size 6 (4mm) needles.
- TAKE TIME TO CHECK YOUR GAUGE.

PROJECT: COWL

- Cast on 101 sts.
- Set-up row (WS) P2, k2, p2, k2, p3, k2, p4, k2, p5, k2, p6, k2, p7, k2, p8, k2, p9, k2, p10, k2, p11, k2, p12.
- Row 1 Sl first st, k the knit sts and p the purl sts.
- Rep row 1 until piece measures approximately 34"/86.5cm from beg.
- Bind off.

FINISHING

- Sew cast-on and bound-off edges tog.

Knit Wits

Use the Internet to find discount yarns and supplies. Knitting websites offer sales on yarn and needles, and free or inexpensive shipping. Be sure to join email lists for promotional offers. eBay, thrift stores, and garage sales are also great places to pick up inexpensive yarn and miscellaneous knitting supplies.

Striped Blanket

Design by Jeannie Chin

MATERIALS

- Approximately 1778 yds of a heavy worsted weight yarn
- Sizes 8 and 9 (5 and 5.5mm) circular needles, 36"/90cm long OR SIZE TO OBTAIN GAUGE
- Size H/8 (5mm) crochet hook (for fringe)

Used in Photo: Montera by Classic Elite Yarns, 3½oz/100g balls, each approximately 127yd/116m (llama/wool). 8 balls in #3862 kingfisher blue (MC). 4 balls in #3845 fieldstone heather (A). 2 balls each in #3826 winter berry (B) and #3822 sunny apricot (C)

MEASUREMENTS

- Approximately 50 x 60"/127 x 152.5cm (excluding fringe)

GAUGE

- 16 sts and 23 rows to 4"/10cm over St st using larger needles.
- TAKE TIME TO CHECK YOUR GAUGE.

NOTE:

1) *The first 2 sts and last 2 sts of each row are worked in garter st throughout, including garter stripe pat.*

2) *Cut colors not in use for more than 4 rows.*

PROJECT: RIDGE STRIPE PATTERN

- With B, 6 rows St st. With C, 2 rows garter st. With B, 5 rows St st.
- Do not turn work. Rejoin C to beg of row to work next row on RS. With C, 2 rows garter st, 5 rows St st, k 1 row on WS. With B, 5 rows St st.
- Do not turn work. Rejoin C to beg of row to work next row on RS. With C, 2 rows garter st.
- Do not turn work. Rejoin B to beg of row to work next row on WS. With B, 6 rows St st.

PROJECT: BLANKET

- With smaller needles and A, cast on 200 sts. Knit 3 rows. Change to larger needles.
- Beg patterns
- With MC, keeping first and last 2 sts in garter st (k every row), work in St st (k on RS, p on WS) for 11 ¾"/30cm.
- With A, work in St st for 3"/7.5cm, end with a WS row.
- Work 34 rows of ridge stripe pat once.
- Beg with a WS row and A, work in St st for 3"/7.5cm.
- Rep from * once more.

LOWER BORDER

- With MC, work in St st for 11¾"/30cm. Change to smaller needles.
- With A, k 3 rows.
- Bind off.

FINISHING

FRINGE

- Cut 150 lengths of B and C each 12"/30.5cm long. *With 3 strands of B held tog, fold in half and with crochet hook, draw loop through a st of border. Pull ends of strands through loop. Beg at one side edge, alternating B and C, add 25 fringes 2"/5cm apart to each border.

Knit Wits

Many knitters keep a journal to record information about projects they've completed—including yarns, needles, and any lessons learned for future projects. A journal is also a good place to keep photos of your finished projects.

Keyhole Bow Tie

Design by Julie Hines

This pretty garter-stitch scarf has bow-shaped ends that tuck through a ribbed tube.

MATERIALS

- Approximately 274 yds of a DK weight yarn
- One pair size 6 (4mm) needles OR SIZE TO OBTAIN GAUGE
- Three size 6 (4mm) double-pointed needles (dpn)

Used in Photo: Organic Wool Naturally Dyed by Rowan Yarns/Westminster Fibers, Inc., 1¾oz/50g skeins, each approximately 137yd/125m (organic wool). 2 skeins in #603 black tea

MEASUREMENTS

- Approximately 5 x 30"/12.5 x 76cm

GAUGE

- 24 sts and 38 rows to 4"/10cm over garter st using size 6 (4mm) needles.
- TAKE TIME TO CHECK YOUR GAUGE.

K1, P1 RIB

- (over an odd number of sts).
- Row 1: k1, p1; rep from * to last st, k1
- Row 2: p1, k1, rep from * to last st, p1.

STITCH GLOSSARY

- Kfb: inc 1 by knitting into the front and back of next st.

BOW TIE

- With size 6 single-pointed needles, cast on 3 sts.
- Next (inc) row Kf-b, k to end.
- Rep last row until there are 30 sts on needle. Work even in garter st (k every row) until piece measures 4½"/11.5cm from beg.

DIVIDE FOR KEYHOLE

- Next row *Sl 1 st to first dpn, sl next st to 2nd dpn; rep from * unt sts are divided equally on 2 dpns.
- Next row With 3rd dpn, work the 15 sts of front dpn in k1, p1 rib for 2"/5cm, end with an inside row
- Cut yarn. 2nd (unworked) dpn is at front. Re-join yarn to 2nd dpn. Work same as for first dpn, end with an outside row.
- Turn work so that working yarn is at back of work.

COMPLETE KEYHOLE

- Next row With single-pointed needle, *k1 from front dpn, k1 fro back dpn; rep from * until all 30 s are on one single-pointed needle
- Work in garter st until piece measures 23½"/59.5cm.
- Work 2nd keyhole same as first. Once all 30 sts have been knitted onto one single-pointed needle, work even in garter st for 3"/7.5cn
- Next (dec) row K1, ssk, k to end.
- Rep dec row until 3 sts rem.
- Next row k3tog.
- Fasten off.
- To wear as shown, pull one end o bow tie through opposite keyhole

Cabled Button Hat

Design by Suvi Simola

The buttons are purely decorative on this clever stockinette hat marked by a twisty cabled band. Shown on page 63

MATERIALS

- Approximately 206 yds of a worsted weight yarn
- One each sizes 6 and 7 (4 and 4.5mm) circular needles, 16"/40cm long OR SIZE TO OBTAIN GAUGE
- Size 7 (4.5mm) double-pointed needles
- Cable needle (cn)
- 16 - ½"/12mm buttons
- Stitch marker

Used in Photo: Chesapeake by Classic Elite Yarns, 1 ¾oz/50g skeins, each approximately 103yd/94m (cotton/ wool). 2 balls in #5904 scuba blue

MEASUREMENTS

- Circumference (at brim) 21"/53.5 cm
- Length 7¼"/18.5cm

GAUGE

- 20 sts and 28 rnds to 4"/10cm over St st using smaller needles.
- TAKE TIME TO CHECK YOUR GAUGE.

STITCH GLOSSARY

- 6-st LC Sl 3 sts to cn and hold to front, k3, k3 from cn.

CABLED BRIM

- With smaller needle, cast on 128 sts, place marker (pm) and join for working in the round, taking care not to twist sts.
- Rnd 1 *k2, p2; rep from * around.
- Rep rnd 1 for k2, p2 rib and work 1 rnd more.
- Next (buttonhole) rnd *k2, p1, yo, k2tog, k1, p2; rep from * around.
- Work 2 rnds in k2, p2 rib.
- Change to larger needle. Next 2 rnds *k6, p2; rep from * around.
- Beg cable pat: Rnd 1 Work 8-st rep 16 times around.
- Work rnds 1-6 of cable 3 times.
- Rep rnd 1 once more.
- Next (dec) rnd *K5, ssk, k2tog, k4, ssk, p1; rep from * around—104 sts. Piece measures approximately 3½"/9cm from beg.
- Purl one rnd for turning ridge.
- Change to smaller needle and work in St st (k every rnd) for 1"/2.5cm.

CABLE PATTERN

- (multiple of 8 sts)
- Rnd 1 *6-st LC, p2; rep from * around.
- Rnds 2-6 K6, p2; rep from * around.
- Rep rnds 1-6 for cable pat.

BODY

- Turn work inside out so WS is facing, cont in St st until piece measures 6"/15cm from turning ridge. (Note A small hole will result at the beg of the rnd from changing directions when you turn the work inside out. This hole will be covered by the brim.)

SHAPE CROWN

Note: Change to dpns when sts no longer fit comfortably on circular needle.

- Rnd 1 *k11, k2tog; rep from * around—96 sts.
- Rnd 2, 4, 6, 8 and 10 Knit.
- Rnd 3 *k10, k2tog; rep from * around—88 sts.
- Rnd 5 *k9, k2tog; rep from * around—80 sts.
- Rnd 7 *k8, k2tog; rep from * around—72 sts.
- Rnd 9 *k7, k2tog; rep from * around—64 sts.
- Rnd 11 *k6, k2tog; rep from * around—56 sts. Cont to dec 8 sts every rnd, working 1 less st before each k2tog, until 16 sts rem.
- Next rnd *k2tog; rep from * around—8 sts.
- Cut yarn and thread through rem sts.

FINISHING

- Turn up brim and sew on buttons to correspond to buttonholes.

Knit Wits

After the band is knit – delineated by a turning ridge – the rest of the cap is turned inside out and worked in the knit stitch.